REEDS
DIESEL
ENGINE
TROUBLESHOOTING
HANDBOOK

D1501346

Other titles in the series:

Reeds Outboard Motor Troubleshooting Handbook
Barry Pickthall
ISBN: 9781408181935

Reeds Skipper's Handbook
For sail and power
6th edition
Malcolm Pearson
ISBN: 9781408124772

Reeds Crew Handbook
For sail and power
Bill Johnson
ISBN: 9781408155714

Reeds Knot Handbook
Jim Whippy
ISBN: 9781408139455

REEDS
DIESEL
ENGINE
TROUBLESHOOTING
HANDBOOK

A POCKET GUIDE TO DIESEL ENGINES

BARRY PICKTHALL

ADLARD COLES NAUTICAL

BLOOMSBURY

LONDON • NEW DELHI • NEW YORK • SYDNEY

Published by Adlard Coles Nautical
an imprint of Bloomsbury Publishing Plc
50 Bedford Square, London, WC1B 3DP
www.adlardcoles.com

First published by Adlard Coles Nautical in 2013

ISBN 978-1-4081-8192-8

A CIP catalogue record for this book is available from the
British Library.

This book is produced using paper that is made from
wood grown in managed, sustainable forests. It is natural,
renewable and recyclable. The logging and manufacturing
processes conform to the environmental regulations of
the country of origin.

Typeset in Gill Sans
Designed by Kayleigh Reynolds/PPL Ltd
Printed and bound in China by C&C Offset Printing Co.

Note: while all reasonable care has been taken in
the publication of this book, the publishers take no
responsibility for the use of the methods or products
described in the book.

CONTENTS

Diesel engines are simpler and safer, as well as being more economical and efficient, than petrol engines. They are at their most efficient when operating at a steady rate, and because they work under high compression, their parts are more robust, which makes them ideal for marine uses.

Regular maintenance is key to reliability. The last thing you want to be doing is crawling around the engine bay when out on the water, so this pocket companion has been written to highlight the regular checks and maintenance needed before and after each trip to keep your diesel engine running as it should.

But if there is a breakdown, this book, which should always be read in conjunction with the engine handbook, offers a simple guide to troubleshooting and provides clear step-by-step instructions to get you going again.

1 HOW A DIESEL ENGINE WORKS

HOW A DIESEL ENGINE WORKS

The diesel engine uses the heat generated by compressing air to ignite fuel sprayed into the combustion chamber through high-pressure injection nozzles. This contrasts with the petrol engine which uses a spark plug to ignite the air/fuel mixture and operates at a much lower compression.

Modern lightweight marine diesel engines are a far cry from previous generations. Engines pre-dating the 1990s, when the electronically managed units first came to prominence, relied on fuel and air being mixed in a pre-combustion chamber

Early diesel engine configuration

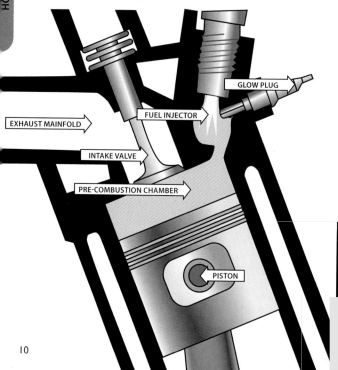

EXHAUST MAINFOLD

FUEL INJECTOR

GLOW PLUG

INTAKE VALVE

PRE-COMBUSTION CHAMBER

PISTON

A Volvo Penta D6 400 lightweight diesel engine equipped with direct injection, an electronic management system and turbocharger.

before injection into each cylinder. The mixing and injection steps were controlled mechanically, which could never match the fuel/air mixture for both fast and slow running. As a result, the fuel 'burn' was often incomplete, particularly at low speeds and fuel wastage and emissions were always high.

The latest diesel engines are managed electronically with ECMs (Electronic Control Modules) and EDCs (Electronic Data Controls) delivering precisely the right amount of fuel the instant it is needed, as well as moderating everything from engine speed and load, piston position, coolant and oil temperature. Fuel is now burned far more efficiently, delivering more power, greater fuel economy, and far lower amounts of carbon dioxide, carbon monoxide, and unburned hydrocarbons.

HOW A DIESEL ENGINE WORKS

The fuel injection pump pressurises fuel into a delivery tube called a rail, and keeps it under constant pressure of 23,500psi or higher, ready for when the ECM determines exactly when - and how much - fuel is to be sprayed through injectors into each cylinder.

With naturally aspirated engines, the air comes through a filter similar to those on petrol engines. Performance orientated diesels are fitted with one and sometimes twin turbochargers designed to ram far greater volumes of air and spent exhaust gases into the cylinders. These turbochargers not only increase power output by 50 per cent or more, but can also improve fuel economy by 20–25 per cent.

AIR FILTER

SECONDARY FUEL FILTER

FUEL TANK

PRIMARY FILTER WITH WATER SEPARATOR

12

JECTORS

VOLVO PENTA

INJECTION PUMP

FUEL FEED PUMP

▬▬▬ Between tank and fuel feed pump = vacuum

▬▬▬ Fuel feed pump to injection pump = pump pressure

▬▬▬ Injection pump to injectors = high pressure

▬▬▬ Return

2 ANATOMY OF A DIESEL ENGINE

ANATOMY OF A DIESEL ENGINE

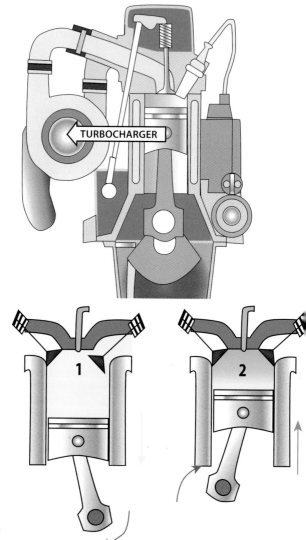

TURBOCHARGER

FOUR-STROKE DIESEL ENGINE CYCLE

1. INDUCTION
The intake valve opens; the piston travels down and draws air into the cylinder.

2. COMPRESSION
The piston travels back up; the highly compressed air rises in temperature.

3. IGNITION / EXPANSION
The diesel fuel injected before the top dead centre spontaneously ignites on contact with the air. The expansion of the gas pushes the piston toward the bottom dead centre.

4. EXHAUST
The exhaust valve opens; the piston travels back up and expels the burnt gas.

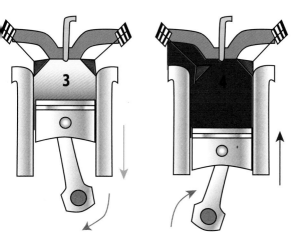

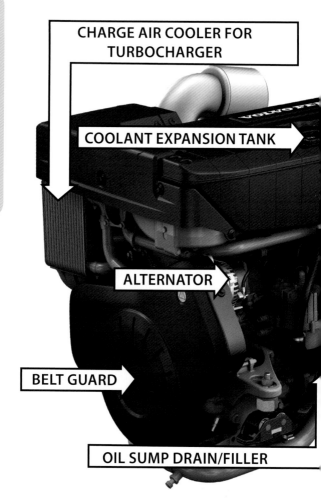

CHARGE AIR COOLER FOR TURBOCHARGER

COOLANT EXPANSION TANK

ALTERNATOR

BELT GUARD

OIL SUMP DRAIN/FILLER

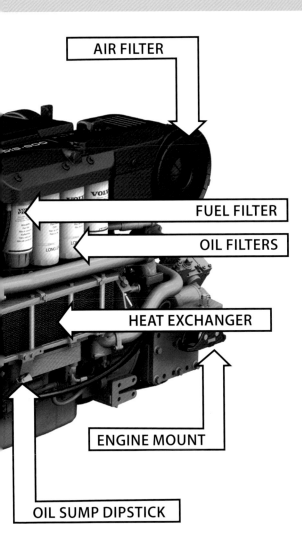

AIR FILTER

FUEL FILTER

OIL FILTERS

HEAT EXCHANGER

ENGINE MOUNT

OIL SUMP DIPSTICK

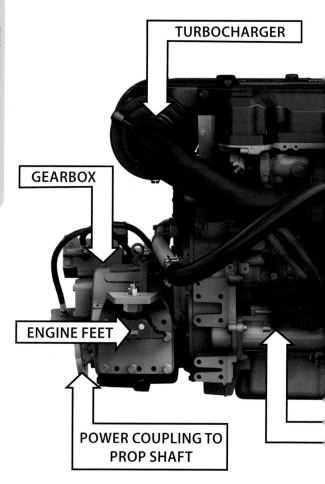

TURBOCHARGER

GEARBOX

ENGINE FEET

POWER COUPLING TO PROP SHAFT

EXHAUST PIPE WITH RISER

ENGINE BLOCK

FUEL INJECTION PUMP

ENGINE FEET

STARTER

DAILY CHECKS

Before you go to sea, ensure that your diesel engine is warmed up and running well before throwing off the warps.

RAW WATER INLET:
- ☐ Check the valve is open and the strainer clear.

DIESEL FUEL FILTER:
- ☐ With a transparent filter, check for water or dirt.
- ☐ Drain off if needed.

ENGINE COMPARTMENT:
- ☐ Take a quick look. Is the bilge clear or are there any oil or water leaks?
- ☐ Check there are no loose wires and that the belts are OK.

ENGINE OIL LEVELS:
- ☐ Check with dipstick.
- ☐ Be careful not to overfill.

START UP:
- ☐ Switch battery power to single battery, so that the operation drains all the power.
- ☐ Check engine oil levels.
- ☐ Ensure gear levers are in neutral.
- ☐ Run at medium revs to warm up.
- ☐ Check that cooling water is running out from the exhaust.

INSTRUMENT PANEL:
- ☐ Are the batteries charging?
- ☐ Is the oil pressure correct?

WHILE THE ENGINE IS RUNNING:
- ☐ Check the stern gland periodically for leaks and tighten grease filter as needed.
- ☐ Check gearbox oil levels and top up with gearbox oil, not engine oil.

Clean the dipstick before checking oil levels.

3 SIMPLE TROUBLESHOOTING

SIMPLE TROUBLESHOOTING

This chart will help pinpoint engine problems.

SYMPTOM	LOW ENGINE COMPRESSION (28)	LOW FUEL PRESSURE (29)	LOW CRANKING SPEED (30)	FAULTY GLOW PLUG OR RELAY (30)	STARVED FUEL SUPPLY (30)	FUEL CONTAMINATION (31)	BLOCKED FUEL SUPPLY (31)	FAULTY DIESEL INJECTORS (32)	FAULTY HIGH-PRESSURE PUMP (32)
POSSIBLE CAUSES									
ENGINE HARD TO START	✓	✓	✓	✓	✓	✓	✓	✓	✓
ROUGH RUNNING AT LOW RPM		✓			✓	✓	✓	✓	✓
LACK OF POWER		✓			✓	✓	✓	✓	✓
DIESEL KNOCK / PINKING						✓	✓	✓	
BLACK SMOKE		✓						✓	✓
WHITE SMOKE	✓	✓		✓	✓	✓		✓	
BLUE SMOKE									

	FAULTY PRESSURE REGULATOR OR SENSOR	FAULTY LOW-PRESSURE PUMP	AIR INTAKE RESTRICTION	TURBO FAILURE	EGR PROBLEMS	LEAKING INJECTORS	FAULTY CAM AND CRANK SENSORS	FAULTY INJECTOR WIRING HARNESS	INTERNAL ENGINE PROBLEMS	PULL-STOP DEVICES
	✓	✓				✓			✓	
	✓	✓	✓			✓	✓	✓	✓	
	✓	✓	✓	✓	✓	✓			✓	
							✓	✓		
			✓	✓	✓	✓	✓	✓		
						✓	✓	✓	✓	
						✓			✓	

SIMPLE TROUBLESHOOTING

CAUSES AND REMEDIES

LOW ENGINE COMPRESSION

Low engine compression occurs when there is not enough heat being produced within the cylinders to ignite the diesel fuel. How to perform a diesel compression test:

1. Ensure batteries are fully charged and that the engine starter motor is in good working condition.
2. Check cylinder head bolts are tightened to correct torque as specified in the handbook.
3. Run engine until the coolant temperature reaches 750–850°C.
4. Remove high pressure injector pipes and lines.
5. Disconnect the fuel shut-off solenoid to disable the fuel injection pump.
6. Remove the No 1 injector, and crank the engine over to clear the gases from the cylinder.
7. Install a compression gauge adapter into the injector hole and connect the compression gauge measurement tool.
8. Crank the engine over for 3–4 seconds and record the compression gauge reading.
9. Repeat steps 7 and 8 for the remaining cylinders.

Engine compression readings should average between 275 and 400 psi, depending on the design and compression ratio, and these readings should not vary more than 10 to 15 per cent (between 30 and 50 psi). If two cylinders have normal pressure readings and two have low readings, engine performance will be reduced. When two cylinders side by side read low, look for a blown head gasket. Where the compression pressure in one cylinder reads low for the first few piston strokes but then increases to normal, this indicates a sticking valve. This can be confirmed by taking a reading from a vacuum gauge.

LOW FUEL PRESSURE

Low fuel pressure is invariably the most common problem with fuel supply. Two faults could cause this:

1. Diesel injectors or the diesel injector rail is leaking.
2. Poor fuel supply to the diesel injectors or diesel injector rail.

Look for faults in three areas:

? Low pressure supply from the fuel tank to the high pressure pump – boats without an electric fuel pump to lift the fuel from the tank to the high pressure pump rely solely on the high pressure pump to lift the fuel from the diesel tank. The bar pressure between the diesel tank and the high-pressure pump should be between 2 and 5 bars.

? The pressure required to deliver fuel from the high-pressure pump to the rail/injectors is approximately 200 bars at cranking speed. This rises to 300 bars at tick-over. At greater rpm levels, the pressure will build to between 1200 and 2000 bars.

? When running at a constant speed, the pressure should remain constant.

SIMPLE TROUBLESHOOTING

LOW CRANKING SPEED

When the engine is cranked over slowly, the diesel pump will not generate enough fuel pressure to initialise fuel injection. This can be one cause for starting problems. Check that the battery is fully charged.

FAULTY GLOW PLUG OR RELAY

Glow plugs are electrically controlled heaters that warm the cylinders and aid cold starting. Without them, a diesel engine will not start because the engine needs hot compressed air to ignite injected diesel. If the glow plugs are faulty the engine will be difficult or impossible to start or, when the engine is cold, it will produce white smoke.

STARVED FUEL SUPPLY

The most common cause of this is cracked or bent fuel pipes.

FUEL CONTAMINATION

Contamination with petrol, water and/or other foreign matter within the fuel can lead to fuel pump and injector failure. The internal parts within the fuel pump and diesel injector get worn and can lead to one or a combination of faults listed in the troubleshooting chart. If you have suffered contamination or had either the diesel injectors or pump exchanged or repaired, clean out the fuel system and replace your fuel filter before fitting the replacement parts.

BLOCKED FUEL SUPPLY

The job of the fuel filter is to remove contaminants from the fuel system before it reaches the diesel injectors or diesel fuel pump. The life cycle of a filter depends on the quality of the fuel passing through it. Normally, the filter is changed during an annual service or seasonally. If the filter becomes clogged before the usual service, then contaminant levels within the fuel are higher than normal.

SIMPLE TROUBLESHOOTING

FAULTY DIESEL INJECTORS

The common cause for injector failure is excessive back flow – the result of a worn pilot valve, nozzles or seals. The faulty parts allow the fuel to travel back up the injector to the fuel system or diesel tank. This leads to a drop in rail pressure which in turn results in poor starting. Worn parts can also cause a delay in the start of injection, which results in rough running at low RPM.

FAULTY HIGH-PRESSURE PUMP

A faulty high-pressure fuel pump will cause low pressure and lead to failure of the fuel pump. The problem often stems from fuel contamination or the fuel pump breaking up internally. This in turn leads to failure of the injectors. Before replacing the high-pressure pump and injectors, clean out the whole fuel system.

FAULTY PRESSURE REGULATOR OR SENSOR

Most engines have a pressure regulator fitted on the diesel high-pressure pump and a sensor on the rail. If either of these become faulty your engine can develop the following issues:
* Hard starting
* Uneven tick-over
* Engine cutting-out when the RPM is increased

FAULTY LOW-PRESSURE PUMP

The low-pressure pump, if one is fitted, will be located either on the fuel pipe near the diesel tank or inside the tank. The symptoms are the same as with a faulty high-pressure pump.

AIR INTAKE RESTRICTION

This will be caused by a blocked air filter or pipe. Some engines are fitted with a butterfly valve, which can sometimes become stuck. Any restrictions in air will cause excessive black smoke and lack of power.

TURBO FAILURE

Turbo problems are invariably caused by:

- Not leaving the engine to idle for a few minutes when it is first started or before switching off.
- Not using the correct oil as specified in the handbook.
- Poor maintenance.

The usual problem is a sticking waste gate, which causes the engine to lose power, smoke excessively or shut down.

If the engine has a variable vane turbo and carbons up, you will experience black smoke, a hesitation on acceleration and lack of power. Check that the sensors and vacuum pipes to and from the inlet, intercooler and turbo are serviceable, and that the clamps are fully tensioned.

EXHAUST GAS RECIRCULATION (EGR) PROBLEMS

The vacuum-controlled EGR valve allows a specific amount of exhaust gas back into the intake manifold, which then mixes with the intake air to cool the combustion process. The exhaust gas also prevents the formation of nitrogen related gases often referred to as NOX emissions. Sometimes the EGR valve can become stuck, causing NOX gases to build up which can lead to rough idling, a loss of power and black or white exhaust smoke.

LEAKING INJECTORS

Leaks around the diesel injectors can lead to:

- Difficulty starting.
- Uneven running.
- Erratic tick-over.
- Black exhaust smoke on acceleration.
- Black tar (carbon) around the injectors.

Diesel injector blowing occurs when the injector seal has not seated correctly in the cylinder head. Try removing the injector, cleaning it and fitting a new copper seal washer. If the escaping combustion gases are eroding the seat within the cylinder head, use a seat-cutting tool to reface the seat.

SIMPLE TROUBLESHOOTING

CAUSES AND REMEDIES

FAULTY CAM AND CRANK SENSORS

The first check is to see if these sensors are cracked, damaged or loose. If in doubt, replace them.

FAULTY INJECTOR WIRING HARNESS

Cam driven injectors (unit injectors) operating under a rocker cover can lead to engine oil coming into contact with the electrical connectors. While diagnostic equipment can indicate faulty injectors, the root cause can often be the injector wiring harness. Before replacing the injectors, check that the electrical connections on the unit injectors have good contact with the wiring harness.

INTERNAL ENGINE PROBLEMS

Starting issues, rough running, a lack of power and blue smoke all indicate internal problems either with a blown head gasket or issues with one or more pistons. Call in a mechanic.

PULL-STOP DEVICES

The most common reason for a boat diesel failing to start relates to when it was last shut down. If it has a 'pull-stop' device (usually a toggle on the end of a 'push-pull' cable), it is easy to forget to push this all the way back after pulling it out to stop the engine.

Make sure the pull-stop knob is pushed all the way home. Engines with electrical stop devices rely on an electrical solenoid, normally located near the injector pump, to do the job. It is a good idea to identify the wiring while everything is working well so that, should the engine fail to fire, you will know where to start looking.

SMOKE SYMPTOMS

WHITE SMOKE
This is a sign that fuel is not being burnt correctly. These are the likely causes:
- Low engine compression
- Fuel contamination
- Pump and engine timing is out of sync
- Fuel starvation to the pump, causing the pump timing to operate incorrectly

BLACK SMOKE
This is caused by an imbalance within the air to fuel ratio. This occurs when the diesel fuel system is delivering either too much fuel into the engine or there is not enough air. These are the likely causes:
- Faulty diesel injectors
- Dirty air filter
- Faulty diesel pump
- Faulty EGR valve
- Faulty intercooler or turbocharger

BLUE SMOKE
This indicates that the engine is burning engine oil. These are the likely causes:
- Faulty diesel injector pump
- Faulty diesel lift pump
- Overfill of engine oil
- Worn piston rings or cylinders
- Faulty valve stem seals or valves

4 FUEL SYSTEM

FUEL SUPPLY PROBLEMS

Problems with the fuel supply are the most common cause of poor running and impromptu stopping.

First check is to see if you have run the tank dry.

Secondly, boats with built-in fuel tanks can also suffer vent problems when salt builds up and blocks the gauze filter in the opening and stops it 'breathing' properly. The salt crystals can usually be scraped away with a sharp knife, but if it is severe there is no option but to replace the vent.

The third most common cause of trouble is fuel contamination.

* Has water got into the fuel?
* Is there any rust or sediment in the tank blocking the filter system, or that has worked its way through to block the fuel injection system?

The first place to check for contamination is the water separator/ fuel filter, usually fitted close to the engine. The original Lucas/CAV filters conveniently have a glass inspection bowl in the bottom of the unit, but these no longer meet EU regulations, and the glass has been replaced with an aluminium bowl, which necessitates a strip-down simply to check for contaminants. If tell-tale globules of water and/or sediment

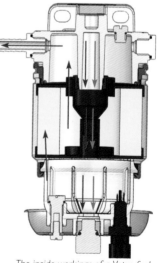

The inside workings of a Vetus fuel filter and water separator

are present then a new filter is the order of the day. Check the secondary fuel filter on the engine too.

To inspect or replace the filter, place a container beneath it to catch the spill. The Lucas/CAV type has a plastic drain screw in the base. Dismantle by undoing the central bolt at the top.

Another type popular in North America is the spin-on fuel/ water separator. Remove it simply by gripping the filter and unscrewing it clockwise when looking from above.

A Lucas/CAV fuel filter/water separator. The water is easily seen as globules in the bottom of the glass bowl

> Remember to remove and replace the rubber ring gaskets each time you take off the filters. Their reuse will invariably lead to leaks.

Changing the filter at least once a year – twice if the boat gets a lot of use – should ensure trouble-free running.

How did water get into the system in the first place? Check the fuel tank. It is not uncommon for water to be present in the tanks on the fuel dock, especially during Spring and Autumn when extremes of temperature can lead to condensation in the storage tanks. The same can happen in the boat tanks too if they are not kept topped up. If water is present, then there is no alternative but to drain down the entire fuel system within the boat.

If the fuel tanks are steel, then water will be corroding the inside of the tank and causing rusty sediment in the bottom. The simple solution here is to replace the tank with a plastic variant and get rid of the problem forever.

FUEL SYSTEM

Take a sample of the fuel from the fuel tank in a clean glass jar from the outlet pipe before it reaches the filter and look at it in a good light. If the fuel is clear and bright then changing the fuel filter should fix the problem. If the fuel is hazy or has particles floating in it, it will block filters and will have to be pumped out and replaced, otherwise the new filter will block up in no time.

COMMON CAUSES OF FILTER BLOCKAGE

Suspended water turns the fuel hazy and is normally a cold season problem. When diesel fuel cools down during storage, dissolved water will be released as small droplets. If the droplets do not drop to the bottom they will form a haze. This can be seen on cold mornings after overnight storage and it will disappear when the fuel warms up. It manifests itself as a greasy emulsion on the filter which disappears when the filter is dried. It can be resolved by ensuring that any settled water is drained from the bottom of the tank each morning.

Suspended particulate matter in the form of dirt, rust or oxidised fuel can form a fine suspension of brown or red particles, causing a greasy black deposit on the fuel filter. Laboratory analysis of the filter and fuel may be required to establish the cause. Resolution of the problem may require the fuel tanks to be emptied

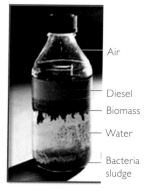

Air

Diesel

Biomass

Water

Bacteria sludge

and cleaned and a change of fuel supplier.

Wax is another problem that can develop in cold conditions, and forms a light yellow suspension in the fuel. This occurs when the fuel is cooled below the temperature at which wax separates from the fuel or cloud point. This forms a yellow waxy deposit which will block filters. This can result from using the incorrect fuel for the season or region, such as summer grade ADF in winter, or bringing an ADF from warmer areas to a colder area during winter. The problem is overcome by adding 30 per cent of heating oil (red diesel) to the fuel and changing the filter.

Fungal contamination, detected as a black/brown mousse blocking filters, is a symptom of poor water draining. It is normally associated with long standing free water, hazy fuel, suspended water and dirt. This is normally a warm season problem and serious contamination will require thorough tank cleaning and treatment with a biocide. Prevention requires a change of filters and frequent checks for water contamination. If the problems persist, change your supplier of fuel.

Changing the main filter

- Turn off the engine and wait until it cools down sufficiently before continuing to the next step.
- Drain water and dirt from the fuel tank. Place the pan under the drain plug, then pull open the drain plug.
- Close the drain plug when the fuel runs clear. Safely dispose of the used fuel.
- Drain water and dirt from the fuel filter. Place the pan under the drain plug, then rotate the plug screw to loosen it until the water and dirt start to stream out.
- Tighten the plug screw, then check the fuel level. Add fuel up to 90 per cent capacity.
- Open the fuel plug on the fuel tank and then use a flat head screwdriver to rotate the air bleeding bolt two or three times.
- Push the fuel priming pump knob and then release it. Continue to prime it until all the bubbles are removed and the fuel looks clear.
- Tighten the air bleeding bolt and close the fuel plug.

BLEEDING THE FUEL SYSTEM

The smallest amount of air in the fuel system can be enough to stop the engine. If you have cleaned or replaced the filter, then it will be necessary to bleed the fuel system through to the injector pumps. The latest engines do this automatically and fresh fuel is pumped through the system simply by pressing the start button and letting the engine prime itself. However, if the engine does not start within 30 seconds you are likely to run the battery flat and will need to bleed the system by hand.

Many systems have hollow 'bleed screws' within the fuel line, but it is also possible to slacken off the pipe union bolts. Start from the fuel tank and work progressively through, slackening off each fitting connection until clear diesel comes out, then retension until you reach the injectors. Once you reach the mechanical fuel pump on the engine, it may be necessary to 'tickle' the finger lever on this lift pump to push the fuel further up the line to the injectors.

1. **Prime filter:** Slacken the bleed screw on the top of the filter and retension once clear fuel comes out.

2. **Engine filter:** Repeat the same. This may be a spin-on filter without a bleed facility. If so, move on the engine fuel pump. Others have the bleed screw just off centre. Don't mistake this for the main bolt that holds the filter in place.

3. **Engine fuel pump:** Operate the finger lever on the lift pump to force the fuel through and up the line to the injectors.

4. **Injectors:** Start with the first in line and slacken the pipe unions either side of the injector. Set the engine to fast idle and use the starter to drive the fuel through, tightening the pipe unions in turn. Don't worry if the engine starts and continues to run on one or two cylinders while the pipe unions are still slack. Just continue down the fuel line until all the injectors are clear of air and the engine is firing on all cylinders.

Bleeding the prime filter.

The bleed screws on the injection pump may require a special spanner. (Below) If the engine has stopped on its own account, it may be necessary to bleed the high pressure injector pipes.

43

FUEL ADDITIVES

In 2011, the sulphur content in heating fuel (red diesel) sold across the European Union was reduced from 1,400pp to 20pp, and the biodiesel mix was increased from 5 to 7 per cent which can increase fungal growth and affect fuel ageing and performance. Australia, Japan and the USA all have different diesel blends, but across the world, the trend is to reduce the sulphur content and attendant emissions.

Sulphur gives diesel its lubricity and natural biocidal action, so the drastic drop in S content, coupled with the increased percentage of biodiesel, which has tracing of water in it, can present an ideal environment for bacteria growth, better known as 'diesel bug'. Various brands of additives are available to counter this. This is what Sirrus Marine, suppliers of OneShot diesel additives, recommend for EU diesel supplies.

DIESEL BUG BIOCIDE: 0.2 LTR – TREATS 200 LITRES

- *Used in spring, summer and autumn*
- Kills & prevents 'diesel bug'
- Inhibits sludge and slime build up
- Prevents plugging of filters, injectors and burners
- Protects against tank and pipe corrosion

DIESEL ANTI-WAX: 0.2 LTR – TREATS 200 LITRES

- *Used in autumn and winter*
- Boosts fuel resistance to waxing and inhibits wax formation
- Very low temperature protection – down to -20°
- Reduces water uptake
- Reduces filter plugging
- Prevents microbiological growth

DIESEL STORAGE PRO: 0.2 LTR – TREATS 800 LITRES

- *Used in autumn and winter*
- Inhibits deposit and varnish build-up
- Disperses sludge and deposits
- Improves long term storage stability

- Inhibits microbiological growth
- Extends the storage life of diesel to up to 2 years

DIESEL FIRST START: 0.2 LTR – TREATS 200 LITRES
- *Used in spring and winter*
- Enhances cold starting
- Enhances warm-up capabilities after prolonged storage
- Reduces smoke & emissions

DIESEL POWER MAX: 0.2 LTR – TREATS 100 LITRES
- *Used in spring, summer and autumn*
- Restores torque & power
- Enhances starting
- Promotes smoother running
- Lowers fuel consumption
- Reduces smoke & emissions
- Cleans internal parts of engine

DIESEL ECO PLUS: 0.2 LTR –TREATS 500 LITRES
- *Used in spring and summer*
- Improves torque & power
- Enhances starting
- Lowers fuel consumption
- Produces lower smoke & emissions
- Reduces sludge, varnishes & deposits
- Inhibits microbial contamination

5 IGNITION SYSTEM

IGNITION SYSTEM

If smoke is being emitted from the engine exhaust, something is not right with the diesel engine. Black, blue or white, take exhaust smoke as a sign that a problem exists. A failure to resolve the problem could shorten the life of the engine and will certainly lead to unnecessary costs.

A diesel engine in good condition should not produce any visible smoke from the exhaust. Older technology engines will produce a short puff of smoke when under initial load because of the lag between when the diesel is injected mechanically into the cylinders and the time when the turbocharger matches the correct air to fuel mix, but this should not happen with modern electronically controlled diesels.

EXHAUST SYSTEMS

The key with any marine exhaust system is that it must not allow water to syphon back into the engine. Some inboard/outdrive installations have this covered by leading the exhaust and cooling through the outdrive leg. The key is to ensure that there is a one-way trap within the exhaust system to stop raw water flowing back from the outlet.

An engine and exhaust system fitted beneath the waterline with a siphon to stop water running back into the engine

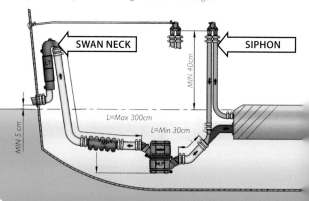

While diesel powered boats have a 'dry' exhaust system where the gases pass through a silencer and out into the atmosphere, most marine installations rely on a 'wet' exhaust system where the engine's cooling water is mixed with the exhaust gas to reduce the temperature and, thus, the chance of a fire. The raw water coolant reduces the gas temperature from around 500°C down to 70°C. This is cool enough for it to pass through reinforced rubber hose piping and plastic mufflers, which withstand the vibrations that build up within a boat much better than a fixed exhaust pipe.

Engine installations set below the waterline are most at risk of leaks and flow-back through the engine, which is why a swan neck or hand-operated gate valve is so important between the exhaust outlet and main exhaust system. Rubber and plastic exhaust systems will give years of service without trouble, but it is important to check for leaks at regular intervals to ensure water and dangerous carbon monoxide gases are not simply leaking into the bilge.

An exhaust system fitted above the waterline does not require a siphon, but the swan neck close to the outlet is imperative

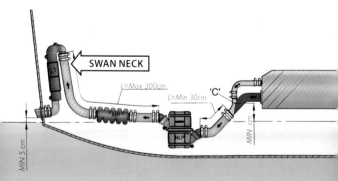

CHECKING VALVE/ROCKER CLEARANCES

This requires a set of feeler gauges in addition to the usual tool kit. If you have not done this before, you may prefer to call in a mechanic.

1. Check in the engine handbook what the valve/rocker clearances should be, and whether these should be adjusted when the engine is at normal running temperature or cold.

2. Remove the rocker cover. Some engines have covers for each cylinder or cylinder groups.

3. Check each valve in turn, both when the gap between rocker head and valve is closed and when it is at its widest aperture.

4. Turn the engine over by hand using the hand-start crank handle or a spanner on the big nut holding the lowest pulley wheel at the front of the engine.

5. Watch for two rockers above one cylinder to 'rock' – when one is on the rise and the other is falling. This indicates that the piston in this cylinder is at the end of its exhaust stroke and commencing its induction stroke.

6. To check the gap, loosen the lock-nut on the rocker, then unscrew the adjuster a couple of turns.

7. Select the correct feeler gauge and push it in the gap between the valve stem and rocker. Adjust the screw to just nip the gauge between the valve stem and rocker.

8. Holding the adjusting screw with a screwdriver, and with the feeler gauge still in place, tighten the lock-nut as before. Once tight, check that the gauge has some resistance within the gap. It should not be jammed tight.

9. Repeat the process for each valve in turn. Check in the handbook for the cylinder firing sequence, or calculate it by adding 1 to the number of cylinders. In the case of a 6-cylinder engine, the magic number will be 7. Subtract the cylinder number you are working on from this magic number (No 1 cylinder is at the flywheel end of the engine) to determine the next in firing order. Thus, if no 2 cylinder is on the rock, 7-2 = 5 shows that no 5 is the next to fire.

10. Once all cylinders have been checked, replace the rocker cover, ensuring that the gasket is seated correctly. If it is damaged, fit a new gasket to avoid oil leakage.

6 STARTING SYSTEM

STARTING SYSTEM

STARTING A DIESEL ENGINE

Diesel engines don't require electricity to start or run, though an electric start facility does take all the hard work out of building up the right amount of compression heat within the cylinders for it to fire.

Engines designed for hand starting have a decompression lever on the top of each cylinder head. These need to be flicked over to release the pressure within each cylinder that will allow you to turn the heavy flywheel sufficiently for the first lever to be closed to get the engine to 'fire' on one cylinder. The other levers are then closed in sequence until all the cylinders are running.

1. Crank the engine over.
2. Once the engine has momentum, flick the first decompression lever closed.
3. As soon as that cylinder fires, close the decompression levers on the other cylinders in sequence until all cylinders are firing.

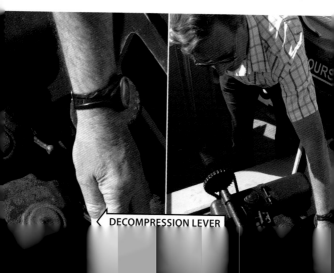

DECOMPRESSION LEVER

ELECTRIC START DIESEL ENGINES

Diesel engines fitted with an electric start have a facility to warm the cylinders prior to starting. In older engines, this will be a glow plug that protrudes through to the pre-combustion chamber. Modern lightweight diesels simply rely on increasing pressure within the cylinder to warm the air. Either way, there is a key setting on the ignition switch to warm the engine prior to engaging the starter motor. The older glow plugs may need as much as 30 seconds to warm up, but with later engines, the time is reduced to just a few seconds. You simply wait for the light to go out on the ignition panel to tell you when to turn the key to start.

1. Turn the ignition key one click to warm the glow plugs to pre-heat the combustion chamber. Most engine control panels have a light which will go out once the air/fuel mix is hot enough to combust.

2. When the pre-heat light goes out, turn the ignition key a second notch to engage the starter motor and fire up the engine.

3. Once running, some engine control units require the ignition key to be turned off and will emit a warning sound until it is.

> To stop the engine, older designs often have a pull-stop knob, often positioned near to the steering position on a yacht. Modern engines have a switch within the ignition system to turn the key to. Once the engine stops, a warning signal then reminds you to then turn the key to the 'off' position and cut the electrical current.

If the engine won't start at all, begin the troubleshooting by looking for the obvious.

If the engine turns over but fails to start:

? Is there a pull-stop knob within the system? Has it been reset?

? Is the fuel tank empty?

? Is the primary filter blocked?

? Is there evidence of water in the separation bowl within the filter?

? If the engine is failing to fire on all cylinders, the likely cause is a blockage within the injector. This may be cleared by bleeding. (see page 42).

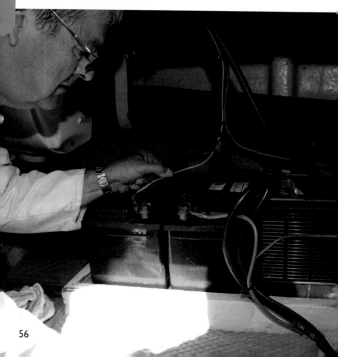

If the engine fails to turn over:

? Are the batteries flat? Many installations have two sets of batteries: one for the engine, the other for the boat. Try turning the battery isolator switch to the boat batteries.

? Is there corrosion on the battery terminals or connectors to the starter motor? This can be enough to restrict power from the battery. Terminals will need to be cleaned with a wire brush, given a coating of battery gel or grease, and the battery re-charged.

AC RECTIFIER TEST

The rectifier is the most common source of problems within the charging system on the boat. These can be caused by a voltage spike, overheating and even a momentary reversal of polarity. Testing the rectifier will require having the workshop manual open to identify the individual wires. Some rectifiers can be tested in-situ, but on others this will have to be tested on the bench. Follow the workshop manual precisely or give the task to the dealer.

STARTING SYSTEM

TESTING THE BATTERIES

1. Check acid levels. If the electroplates are visible, top up with de-ionised (distilled) water.

2. Check the voltage reading using a multimeter across the positive and negative terminals. To ensure accurate results, this test needs to be performed several hours after the battery was last used or topped up, and with all inboard systems turned off.

OPEN CIRCUIT VOLTAGE TEST

REMAINING CHARGE	VOLTAGE READING*
100 per cent	12.6+
75 per cent	12.4
50 per cent	12.2
25 per cent	12
0 per cent	11.7-

*gel batteries will read higher than wet cell batteries

BATTERY CAPACITY/DRAIN TEST

This is best tested by removing the battery and taking it to your dealer who will quickly ascertain whether the unit has reached the end of its life.

TROUBLESHOOTING CHARGING SYSTEM PROBLEMS

SYMPTOM	CAUSE/SOLUTION
VOLTMETER ON INSTRUMENT PANEL UNDER-READING	Fault within charging system. Call in dealer to test entire system.
BATTERY REQUIRES CONSTANT TOP UPS	Faulty regulator overcharging battery, or battery at end of its life

SYMPTOM	CAUSE/SOLUTION
LIGHTING BRIGHTNESS INCREASES WITH ENGINE REVS	Faulty regulator overcharging. Three step voltage check is a simple way to verify engine charge rate and also highlights problems with the regulator if one is fitted.

Turn off systems on the boat, then turn on the ignition switch.

1. Using the voltmeter, take a direct reading from the battery terminals to establish a base voltage.

2. Start the engine and set it to run at 1,000 rpm. Take a fresh battery reading. The voltage reading should increase by 1–3 volts. If it is more, then the rectifier is faulty and will need to be replaced. If there is no increase in unloaded voltage, then there is no charge coming from the engine.

3. With the engine still running at 1,000 rpm, turn on all electrical accessories. Take a new battery reading. The voltage should drop to no less than 0.5v of your base voltage.

This is your regulated voltage. If the reading is less than 0.5v, then engine charging system or alternator does not have sufficient amperage capacity for your boat. Your dealer should be able to supply a replacement heavy duty alternator or stator set.

BATTERY MAINTENANCE

Any corrosion within the wiring system on a boat spells trouble. Corrosion around the battery terminals and leads, particularly so. All electrical connections need to be kept clean and tight because corrosion and loose connections lead to shorting out, battery drain and blown fuses. Look at your batteries regularly:

- Turn off the main battery switch.
- Loosen the clamps holding the red (positive) and black (negative) cables to the battery posts and twist to remove them.
- Wash down the battery posts with plenty of hot water to flush away any acidic crystals.
- Clean the terminal posts with a wire brush or emery paper, being careful not to short out the two terminals.
- Smear the terminal posts with petroleum jelly to prevent moisture and replace the terminals, widest diameter down on their correct + - posts. Re-tighten the clamp bolts.
- Smear more petroleum jelly over the whole terminal.

Modern marine batteries are sealed 'maintenance free' units, but older designs require regular topping up with de-ionised water which over time evaporates from within the cells. To check these:

- Unscrew the filler cap on each cell and inspect the level of acid, which should just cover the top of the electrolyte plates.
- If any of the cells are dry, replenish the acid with de-ionised water. Do not overfill.
- Wipe away any water spillage.

Some batteries have special fillers designed to minimise the loss of acid. Instructions for topping up will be found on the battery casing.

If the boat is left unused for any length of time, such as during the winter layup, the batteries should be left fully charged, but with their terminals disconnected. This is particularly important if the temperature is likely to drop below freezing.

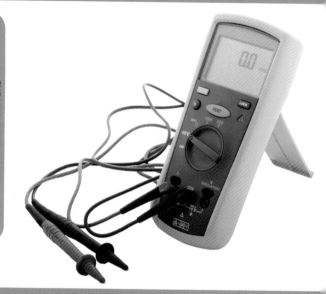

ELECTRIC STARTERS

Inboard engines are commonly fitted with an inertia starter. These rely on the spinning starter motor 'throwing' the drive cog upwards to engage with the teeth around the flywheel ring gear. The most common problem is that the starter spins too slowly to engage with the flywheel. This can be caused by:

1. Low battery power.

2. Corroded or loose wiring terminals.

To check the battery, perform an open circuit voltage test (see page 58).

If the battery is low, recharge or replace it.

Once the battery is fully charged, check that the black grounding plate from the battery is free from corrosion and bolts are tight. Now check the voltage readings with a multimeter at the following points within the starter circuitry.

1 Input lead from battery to starter button/solenoid: the reading should be almost identical to the direct reading across the battery. If not then this suggests a bad connection or broken wire between battery and solenoid.

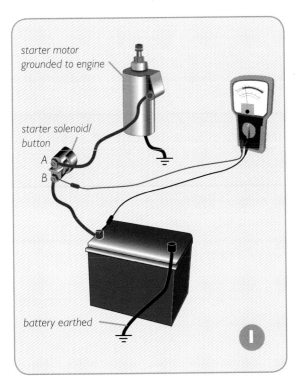

starter motor grounded to engine

starter solenoid/ button

A

B

battery earthed

VOLTAGE CHECK AT STARTER BUTTON/SOLENOID

2 Output lead from starter button: first disable the
ignition system so that the engine does not fire up during
the following four tests. Turn key or press the starter button
while pressing the red test probe against the output lead.
If the reading is less than 12 volts the problem is likely to
be within the starter button/solenoid. Replace with a new
button.

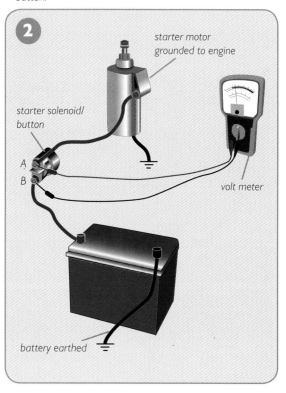

starter motor
grounded to engine

starter solenoid/
button

A

B

volt meter

battery earthed

VOLTAGE DROP TEST BETWEEN SOLENOID AND STARTER MOTOR

3 Input lead to neutral safety switch: turn key or press the starter button. The reading should not exceed 0.2 volts. If it does, the connection to the starter motor may be corroded or the cable too thin. This should be the same size as the battery cables.

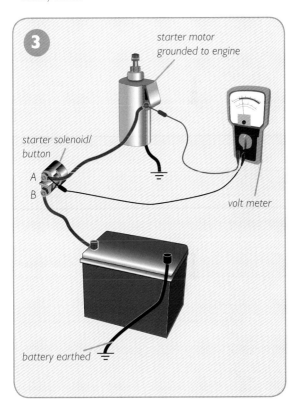

starter motor
grounded to engine

starter solenoid/
button

A

B

volt meter

battery earthed

VOLTAGE DROP TEST BETWEEN BATTERY AND STARTER MOTOR

4 Output lead from neutral safety switch: first check that the gear lever is set to neutral, then turn key or press the starter button. If the reading is above 0.3 volts, there is either a bad connection at the engine or the negative battery post, or the cable is undersized.

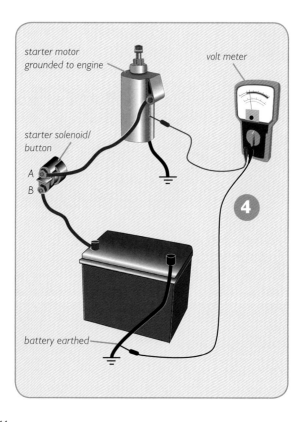

starter motor
grounded to engine

volt meter

starter solenoid/
button

A

B

4

battery earthed

INTERGRATED CIRCUIT VOLTAGE TEST

5 Set the gear lever to neutral, turn on the ignition and check the voltage across each section of the circuit in turn. Input lead to starter motor: if the readings are less than 12 volts (or fail to match the reading from across the two battery terminals), there will be corrosion or a broken wire between point 4 and 5. Repair or replace. If there is 12 volts reaching point 5, but the starter motor does not work, then the problem is with this motor which will require specialist repair or replacement.

Modern remote control systems are now very complex. Checking the starter switch, neutral switch or even the cabling between them can require specialist knowledge and is best left to the dealer to test.

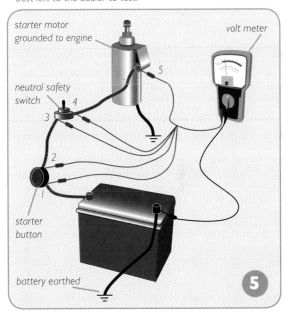

starter motor grounded to engine

volt meter

5

neutral safety switch

4

3

2

1

starter button

battery earthed

5

DRIVE BELTS

Should a drive belt break at sea, the engine is likely to lose circulation of coolant and overheat almost immediately. You may also lose the charge to the batteries. Having spare belts onboard is a get-you-home essential, but checking the belts regularly for wear and tear is all part of the 'stitch-in-time' maintenance philosophy that could save you the sickening task of having to work on the engine at sea.

On many engines, the crankshaft pulley belt drives the water pump and alternator. If the belt is too slack, it will slip and the engine is likely to overheat. The telltale noise is a screeching sound. If the belt is too tight, then the side load this exerts on the bearings within the alternator and water pump will lead to increased wear and early breakdown.

Get into the routine of inspecting the belt and tension each time you check the oil levels in the engine.
- Look for cuts, fraying and any traces of oil that could lead to the rubber perishing.
- Check the tension by pushing down on the belt mid-way between two of the pulleys. It should not deflect more than ½ inch (13mm).

TO ADJUST THE BELT OR REPLACE IT
- Loosen the bolts holding the alternator to the engine.
- Slacken the bolt on the slide adjuster.

TO REPLACE THE BELT

- Push the alternator towards the engine to release the old belt.
- Clean any oil residue from the pulleys, remove rust and loose paint with a wire brush, and repaint.

FITTING A NEW BELT AND ADJUSTING ITS TENSION

1. Start by putting the belt on the crankshaft pulley, then around the water pump and idler wheel if there is one, before guiding it into place over the alternator pulley. If necessary, use a large screwdriver to lever the belt onto the first part of the pulley, taking care not to damage the belt.

2. Use a spanner on the retaining nut holding the crankshaft pulley and, turning it clockwise with one hand, steer the belt onto the alternator pulley with the other.

3. Use a large screwdriver or the handle of a hammer to lever the alternator away from the engine block until the belt is tensioned correctly, then tighten the bolt on the slide adjuster.

4. Re-tighten the other bolts holding the alternator to the engine block mount.

5. Run the engine to test, and recheck the tension after a few hours.

7 COOLING SYSTEM

COOLING SYSTEM

Marine engine installations have either a 'direct' or 'indirect' cooling system. The 'direct' cooling system relies on raw water being sucked in from an inlet skin fitting below the waterline to a raw water filter that guards against weed or particles blocking up the system, and on to the raw water pump fitted on the engine. This then pushes the water

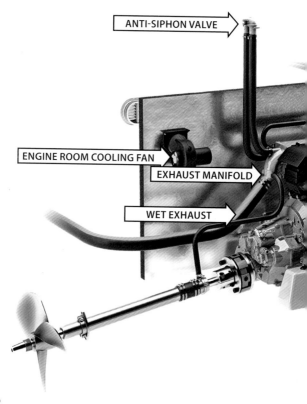

ANTI-SIPHON VALVE

ENGINE ROOM COOLING FAN

EXHAUST MANIFOLD

WET EXHAUST

through an oil cooler (if fitted) and onwards through the cooling system pipework within the engine block before exiting, via a thermostat, either directly to an outlet skin fitting through the side of the hull, or, most commonly, out through the exhaust system where the water is used to cool the exhaust gases. An anti-siphon valve built into the exhaust manifold just before the injection bend is usually fitted to reduce the risk of cooling water flooding back into the engine.

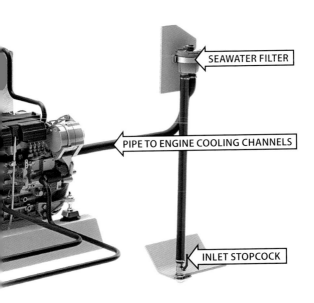

SEAWATER FILTER

PIPE TO ENGINE COOLING CHANNELS

INLET STOPCOCK

This is a very simple system, but the engine is susceptible to corrosion, especially when operating in sea water. Zinc anodes can combat the problem but will need to be replaced regularly. Check in the engine manual for where they are fitted and their recommended replacement period.

The indirect cooling system reduces the risk of corrosion by having an enclosed fresh water circulation system running through the engine. This provides better control over the engine's operating temperature range, which is maintained by passing the coolant through a heat exchanger. This acts very much like a radiator, except that it is a flow of raw water through the heat exchanger, rather than air, that cools the enclosed fresh water. A header tank, often combined within the heat exchanger on top of the engine, provides a reserve supply of coolant and acts as the expansion and contraction vessel.

As with the 'direct' cooling system, the raw water follows the same path, being sucked in from an inlet skin fitting below the waterline to a raw water filter and on to the raw water pump fitted on the engine. This then pushes the water through an oil cooler (if fitted) and onwards through the heat exchanger before exiting through the exhaust system.

EARLY SYMPTOMS OF OVERHEATING
- Loss of power.
- Burning smell.
- 'Pinking' noise from the engine.
- Paint discolouration around the power head.

Stop the engine immediately and check out the cause. Continued use is likely to lead to seizure, or at the very least, a cracked or warped head and blown gaskets.

LIKELY CAUSES
- Obstruction to water flow.
    - **?** Is the water inlet stopcock open?
    - **?** Is weed or plastic blocking the inlet skin fitting?

- Is the raw water filter blocked?
  - **?** Faulty thermostat. Remove and test in pot of water on stove (see below).
  - **?** Faulty water pump or impeller (see page 80).

TESTING THE THERMOSTAT

If water is entering the cooling system but the flow is not matched at the outlet port, a sticking thermostat is a likely cause.

- Remove the bolts holding the cover.
- Pull thermostat from cavity and clean the thermostat with a wire brush.
- Place thermostat in pot of fresh water and heat on stove.
- Monitor water temperature with a cooking thermometer.
- If thermostat does not open at the requisite temperature listed in the handbook, replace it.
- When refitting the thermostat cover, always replace the gasket to avoid the possibility of leaks splashing on the ignition system.

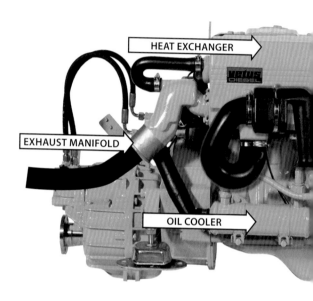

HEAT EXCHANGER

EXHAUST MANIFOLD

OIL COOLER

INDIRECT COOLING SYSTEM

- Check the raw water feed (as above).
- Does the header tank need topping up?
- Are there signs of water seepage around the head? This could indicate a blown head gasket or warped head. This is best left to the dealer or a mechanic to sort out.
- Are there signs of water seepage around the header tank cap? These caps soon corrode and can fail either because the sealing ring is damaged or because the spring is 'tired'. These are cheap to replace and you should do so even if the signs point to problems with the head. A new cap could be all that is needed to solve water loss and save a great deal of worry and expense.

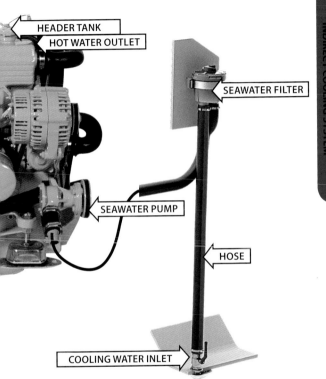

HEADER TANK

HOT WATER OUTLET

SEAWATER FILTER

SEAWATER PUMP

HOSE

COOLING WATER INLET

DAILY CHECKS

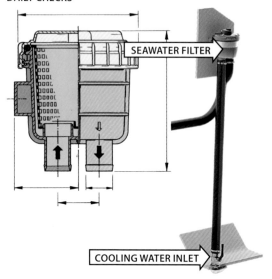

SEAWATER FILTER

COOLING WATER INLET

CLEARING THE RAW WATER FILTER

This should be checked each day. If the filter has a transparent top, you should be able to see the water bubbling through and any particles trapped in the filter. To clear the filter:

- Close the seacock.
- Remove the cover.
- Remove the filter element and clean.
- Refit the filter, making sure that it is seated properly.
- Refit the cover, making certain that it is screwed down tight.
- Re-open the seacock and check for leaks. If there are, repeat the process.
- REMEMBER TO TURN THE SEACOCK BACK ON BEFORE STARTING THE ENGINE.

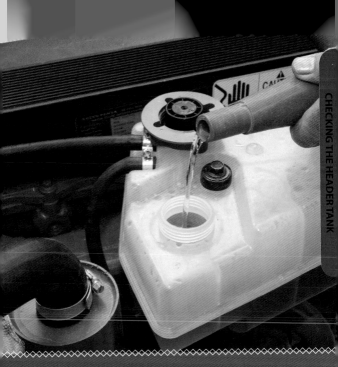

CHECKING THE HEADER TANK

- Remove the header tank cap. If the engine is hot, cover the cap with a towel to avoid scalding, and unscrew the cap slowly to release the pressure. Some caps need to be pushed down before twisting them to release.
- Check the water level. The header acts as an expansion tank so don't over-fill it. The tank may have a water level marked on it, otherwise check the engine handbook. In practice, if you can just touch the water with your finger, it should be full.
- Refill with fresh water mixed with antifreeze.
- Replace the cap.

I.

WATER PUMP SERVICE

The water pump impeller is likely to be damaged if the raw water pump runs dry. If the engine shows any signs of overheating, the impeller may need to be replaced. Purchase a replacement impeller kit which will come with a new gasket.

I. Remove the front plate of the pump and clean off remnants of the paper gasket from both the plate and housing.

2

2. Prise out the impeller with pliers or two screwdrivers, taking care not to damage the body of the pump.
3. Remove any broken pieces. If the impeller has disintegrated completely, check for pieces in the pipework leading to the heat exchanger and remove.

3

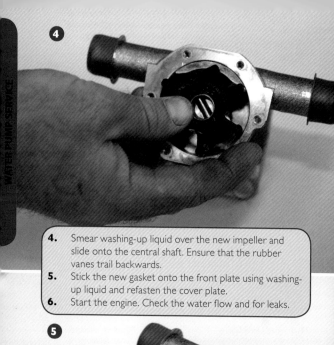

4. Smear washing-up liquid over the new impeller and slide onto the central shaft. Ensure that the rubber vanes trail backwards.

5. Stick the new gasket onto the front plate using washing-up liquid and refasten the cover plate.

6. Start the engine. Check the water flow and for leaks.

8 LUBRICATION SYSTEM

LUBRICATION SYSTEM

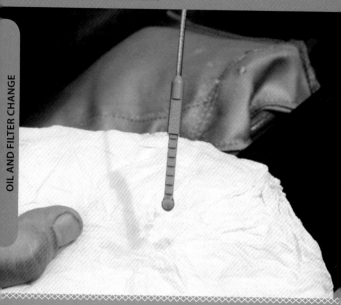

Oil is the lifeblood within any engine. Check the dipstick each day you use the boat, and keep the engine topped up.

1. Stop the engine if it has been running and leave for 5 minutes to allow the oil to return to the sump.
2. Pull the dipstick, wipe with a clean cloth or kitchen roll and re-insert it, ensuring that the stick is pushed fully home.
3. Remove the stick again and check the oil level. It should be somewhere between the 'min' and 'max' lines.
4. Re-insert the dipstick.
5. If the reading is near or below 'min', top up the engine by pouring a measure of oil through the filler cap, which is usually located on the rocker cover.
6. Leave for 1 minute to allow the oil to drain down then re-check the level.
7. Never overfill.

OIL AND FILTER CHANGE

The oil and filter should be changed every 200 hours or at the start of each season. Always change the filter whenever changing the oil.

CHANGING THE OIL FILTER

* Run the engine for 5 minutes to get the oil up to temperature.

* Remove spin-on filter by unscrewing it with a purpose-made strap or chain wrench. As a last resort, hammer a large screwdriver through the canister and use it as a lever, but not before putting down plenty of cloth or paper to soak up the oil that will spill down.

- To replace, fit new O rings that come with the filter (never refit the old seals), smearing a thin film of fresh oil around the face to hold the seal in place.
- Spin the filter on until the sealing ring is just pinched between filter and engine, then tighten a further half turn by hand. Never over-tighten it.
- If your engine has a cartridge filter, this is secured in place by a bolt running through the centre of the filter.
- Remove the old seal from the filter head and replace the cartridge, using new seals supplied. Ensure that any springs and washers are replaced into their correct order and the filter is fitted the right way up.
- Smear fresh oil around the O ring and check that this is seated properly before tensioning up. Again, resist over-tightening the retaining bolt because the pressure could split the seal.

CHANGING ENGINE OIL

Some engines are fitted with a sump pump. Others are supplied with a stirrup pump, fitted with a small bore plastic pipe to insert down the dipstick hole. Whichever, check in the handbook how much oil should be in the engine and ensure that you have a container large enough to collect it all. If a pump is not available, then there is no alternative but to remove the sump drain plug. Hopefully there is enough room under the engine to insert a container to catch the oil, otherwise it will make an unholy mess in the bilge.

REMEMBER TO REPLACE THE SUMP DRAIN PLUG ONCE THE OIL HAS DRAINED OUT.

Pour in a measured amount of the correct grade of oil as specified in the engine handbook, being careful not to spill any over the engine. Wipe up any spillage immediately. Replace the filler cap and run the engine in neutral gear at tick-over speed for 5 minutes, then check to see if there are any leaks. If so, you will need to remove the filter and ensure that the seals are seated correctly.

9 DRIVE SYSTEM

DRIVE SYSTEM

DRIVE SYSTEM

A propeller operates at its optimum performance at around 1,000 rpm and below. Since modern diesel engines can rev at four times this speed, the drive system includes a reduction gear to reduce shaft speed. This is invariably incorporated into the gearbox to give the drive system a forward and reverse capability. The reduction gear also has the benefit of increasing torque or the turning force on the propeller.

There are various reduction gear systems – the simple gearbox, the layshaft and epicyclical. They all have one thing in common – oil. Check the handbook for which type of oil your gearbox requires: automatic transmission fluid, gear oil or monograde engine oil. These oils should never be mixed.

The gearbox is fitted close to the drive shaft coupling at the rear of the engine, and is rarely as easy to service as the engine. Gearboxes don't use oil as an engine does, but it is necessary to check visually for leaks on a regular basis, and to draw the dipstick at least once a month.

The dipstick can be in an awkward spot. Ensure that it is put back fully home and does not leak oil once the engine is running.

Rigid Assembly

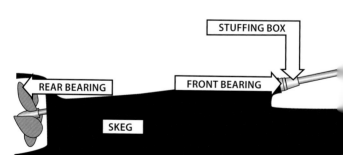

Flexible Assembly

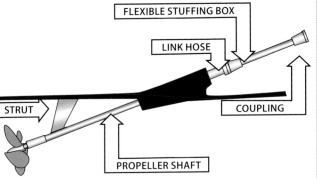

TO CHECK THE OIL LEVEL

- Turn the engine off.
- Draw the dipstick and wipe with a clean cloth.
- Push the dipstick back down its hole – check in the handbook to see if it must be screwed back in place to give an accurate level.
- Draw the dipstick again and check the oil level.
- Top up with a measured amount of the correct oil (check the handbook) through the filler cap if there is one, or through the dipstick hole.
- NEVER OVERFILL.
- Return the dipstick down its hole.
- Clean up any residue.

STERN GLAND

The stern gland is situated at the inboard end of the stern tube and provides a waterproof seal around the propeller shaft. There are three types of seal: the stuffing box, the diaphragm and lip seal.

STUFFING BOX

This holds a reservoir of grease, which acts in conjunction with fibrous packing, as both a lubricant and seal. This system relies on pressure to maintain the seal. This is achieved by tightening the cap or screw one turn for every four hours of running. If it is left unattended, then the stuffing box will begin to weep water into the bilge. Eventually, the grease reservoir will need to be replenished.

- Unscrew the top cap or plunger.
- Invert the grease can over the cap opening, ensuring that the central hole within the retaining disc within the can is directly over the greaser.
- Press the can downwards forcing the retaining disc down into the can, and the grease out into the stuffing box cap. Stop a few times to allow trapped air within the stuffing box to escape.
- Once full, replace the cap on the stuffing box and tighten down.
- Wipe clean any residue.

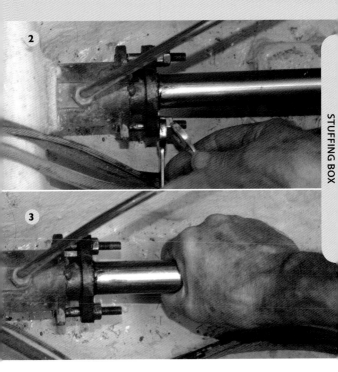

TO ADJUST THE STUFFING BOX

1. Stop the engine, set gear to neutral and turn the shaft by hand to gauge the level of friction.
2. Slacken off the locking nuts holding the two parts of the stern gland together, and then tighten the clamping bolts a half turn at a time.
3. Turn the shaft by hand to check for friction and drips of water. The shaft should still turn freely and water ingress should be no more than 6 drips per minute. If it is leaking more than this, tighten the clamping bolts half a turn at a time until the leak is reduced.
4. Once adjusted, retighten the locking nuts.

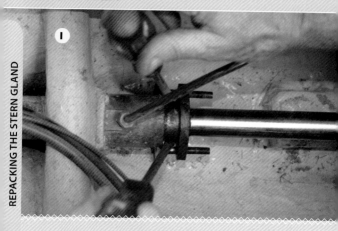

REPACKING THE STERN GLAND

When the stuffing box cannot be adjusted enough to reduce the ingress of water, without making the shaft difficult to turn by hand, then it is time to replace the fibrous packing material within the gland. THIS CAN ONLY BE DONE WITH THE BOAT LIFTED OUT OF THE WATER.

1. Slacken off the locking nuts holding the two parts of the stern gland together and remove the clamping bolts. Use two screwdrivers to prise the outer plate from the gland.
2. Remove the old packing material with a sharp screwdriver or coat-hanger wire.
3. Clean stern gland and shaft with a degreasing agent such as 'Gunk' or 'Jizer', then wipe with a clean cloth.

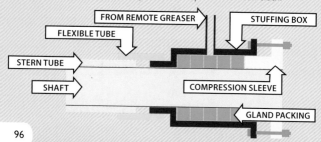

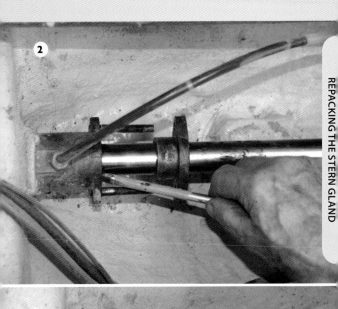

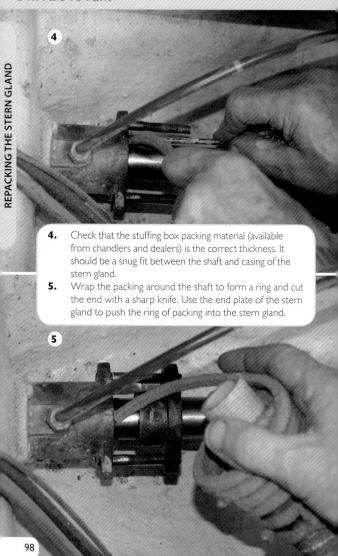

4. Check that the stuffing box packing material (available from chandlers and dealers) is the correct thickness. It should be a snug fit between the shaft and casing of the stern gland.

5. Wrap the packing around the shaft to form a ring and cut the end with a sharp knife. Use the end plate of the stern gland to push the ring of packing into the stern gland.

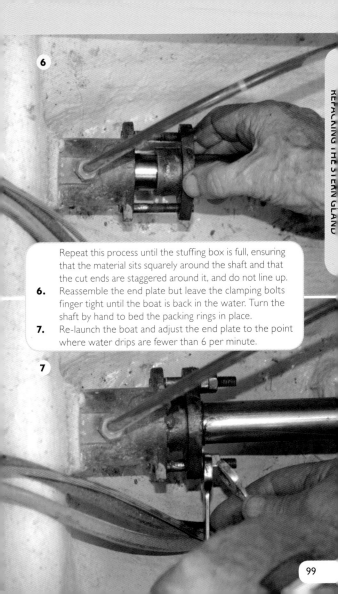

6

Repeat this process until the stuffing box is full, ensuring that the material sits squarely around the shaft and that the cut ends are staggered around it, and do not line up.

6. Reassemble the end plate but leave the clamping bolts finger tight until the boat is back in the water. Turn the shaft by hand to bed the packing rings in place.

7. Re-launch the boat and adjust the end plate to the point where water drips are fewer than 6 per minute.

7

DRIVE SYSTEM

RUBBER DIAPHRAGM SEAL
The diaphragm seal is a modern replacement for the traditional stuffing box. It has the advantage of being self-aligning, dripless and doesn't need regular adjustment. I have had one fitted on my yacht for ten years without experiencing any problems or leaks.

The spring-loaded rubber diaphragm is clamped to the stern tube with a jubilee clip and has a ceramic or carbon shaft-sealing ring moulded in at the other end which remains in firm contact with a stainless steel collar on the shaft.

The only maintenance required is a periodic check for splits in the rubber diaphragm, and a tug on the collar to pull it away from the shaft seat, to vent out any air whenever the boat is re-launched and flush out any debris that might enter through the cutlass bearing at the outer end of the prop shaft.

The diaphragm seal requires 'burping' - pulling back the rubber gland - to release all air out of the gland, each time the boat is launched. This particular stern gland seal has been in the boat for more than 12 years and has never leaked.

LIP SEAL

Lip shaft seals come in various forms:

- A simple synthetic rubber sleeve with lip seals moulded on the inner side, providing a waterproof seal around the shaft.
- Flexible rubber bellows that hold a reservoir of oil.
- Flexible rubber bellows that rely on water injection to minimise friction.

The oil lip seal needs to be topped up every 200 hours or once a season. The water lip seals simply need to be vented each time the boat is re-launched to ensure that the bellows remain full of water.

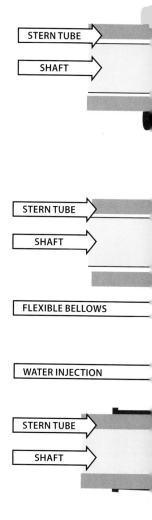

STERN TUBE

SHAFT

STERN TUBE

SHAFT

FLEXIBLE BELLOWS

WATER INJECTION

STERN TUBE

SHAFT

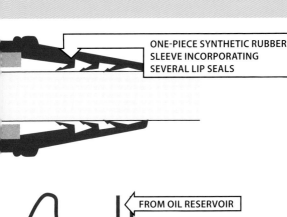

ONE-PIECE SYNTHETIC RUBBER
SLEEVE INCORPORATING
SEVERAL LIP SEALS

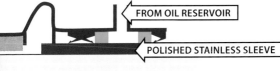

FROM OIL RESERVOIR

POLISHED STAINLESS SLEEVE

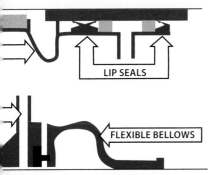

LIP SEALS

FLEXIBLE BELLOWS

EAT

SEALING RIG

DRIVE SYSTEM

CUTLASS BEARING

This is the outer bearing supporting the end of the propeller shaft, and set inside the end of the stern tube or within a supporting strut close to the propeller. Usually moulded from a hard rubber nitrile, the longitudinal flutes allow water to lubricate the shaft and flush out any grit or other hard material that might cause wear on the shaft. The outer shell of the bearing is either bronze or a non-metallic composite for use with aluminium struts or stern tubes where corrosion could be a problem.

Though durable, these bearings do wear out, and must be replaced to avoid vibrations, which can lead to shaft or strut damage. The symptoms are:

- A constant rumbling or vibration that slowly increases over time.
- Movement in the shaft when waggling the propeller up and down. The maximum tolerance between the shaft and bearing surface are as in the table.

SHAFT DIAMETER	MAX TOLERANCE
1 inch shaft (25.4mm)	0.005 inch (0.127mm)
1.25 inch shaft (31.75mm)	0.007 inch (0.178mm)
1.5 inch shaft (38.1mm)	0.009 inch (0.228mm)

Removing the cutlass bearing can be challenging, particularly when installed in the stern tube rather than in a strut, so you may wish to call in a marine engineer who will have the experience to also check alignment of the engine and shaft. Should you wish to do it yourself, this is the routine for replacing the cutlass bearing:

REMOVING THE PROP SHAFT

- Remove any setscrews or locking nuts that may be used to secure the shaft to the coupling at the transmission. Locking nuts are located inside the coupling and can only be exposed by first separating the coupling from the transmission.
- Withdraw the shaft using a shaft puller or slide hammer.
- Loosen the setscrews that hold the cutlass bearing in place.
- Cut through the rubber nitrile bearing along one of the flutes with a soft wood saw blade, being careful not to damage the bearing shell.
- Gently drive a screwdriver between the rubber and the bearing shell until you can grip the rubber with pliers, then twist and pull to extract the bearing.

TO INSTALL A NEW BEARING

- Use liquid soap on the outside of the rubber and tap it in place using a block of soft wood and a mallet.
- Reinstall the bearing setscrews using Loctite or similar thread-locking glue.
- Reinstall the propeller shaft.

DRIVE SYSTEM

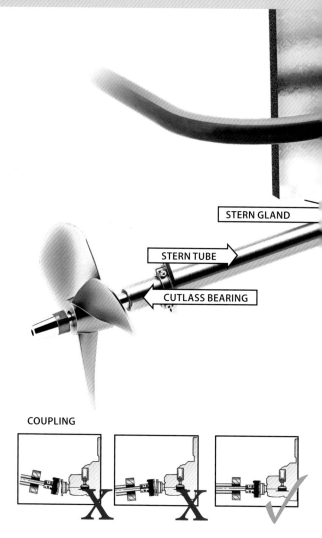

STERN GLAND

STERN TUBE

CUTLASS BEARING

COUPLING

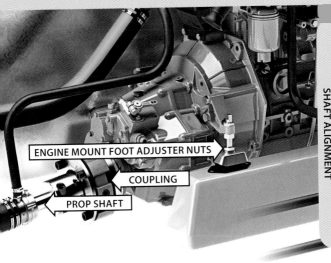

ENGINE MOUNT FOOT ADJUSTER NUTS

COUPLING

PROP SHAFT

SHAFT ALIGNMENT

Correct alignment of the engine and drive shaft is vital. If the coupling is out of line, then this will lead to undue vibration, and excessive wear within the cutlass bearing. To check alignment:

- Select neutral gear.
- Rotate the propeller shaft by hand and check for any anomaly between the shaft and gearbox coupling.
- Adjust the engine mounts to bring the gearbox shaft into approximate line with the shaft. Make sure that the engine is being supported equally on each mount, and not simply diagonally, otherwise the engine will vibrate excessively when running.
- Fine-tune the alignment by inserting a feeler gauge between the coupling plates. The maximum tolerance is 0.005mm per centimeter of the coupling's diameter.
- Once you are satisfied that the engine and propeller shaft are in line, tighten the locking nuts on the engine mounts and the coupling.

SAILDRIVES

Saildrives, or S-Drives as they are also known, provide an efficiently shaped outdrive leg for sailboats. Manufacturers like Volvo recommend that the rubber gasket waterproofing the through-hull assembly be replaced every 7 years, and since it sits below the waterline, this is a sensible precaution. Removing the engine and dismantling the Saildrive to fit a new gasket is a task best left to a reputable marine engineer, so the advice below is limited to annual servicing of these units.

LAYING-UP

When hauling out for antifouling or laying-up, the Saildrive leg requires a high-pressure wash before it has a chance to dry out, in order to remove any weed or crustaceans.

If the boat is to be left out for an extended period:
- Spray penetrating oil into the gap between shaft and leg.
- Waggle the propeller to see if there is any play in the shaft. If so, consult a marine engineer.
- Check the anode. If this is badly corroded, plan to replace it before re-launch.

SAILDRIVE ANNUAL SERVICE

The latest Saildrives allow for an oil change to be performed from inside the boat. This is achieved with a vacuum pump fitted to a narrow tube pushed down the dipstick hole.

The first check should be the condition of the oil. If it is milky, this indicates that the waterproof seal needs to be replaced. Another task for the marine engineer.

With some Saildrive installations, extracting the oil from the leg can be a problem. Sometimes it is only possible to remove the top third of the contents. This is because the pipe is either too stiff to bend around the gears, or too short to reach the bottom of the casing. One solution is to suck out what you can, replace with fresh oil, and run the engine for a few minutes, before repeating the operation until the dipped oil is clean. This may need to be done 8–10 times before the oil is fully replaced.

Check the handbook as to what grade of oil to use. In 2010, Volvo Penta issued a bulletin recommending a switch from ATF fluid in their Saildrives to SAE 15W40 oil, so a check on the manufacturer's website for the latest information would be prudent.

The propeller should also be removed at least once a season to check for shaft wear and for any fishing line caught around the hub – the usual cause of seal failure. Grease the shaft to prevent corrosion before re-installing the propeller.

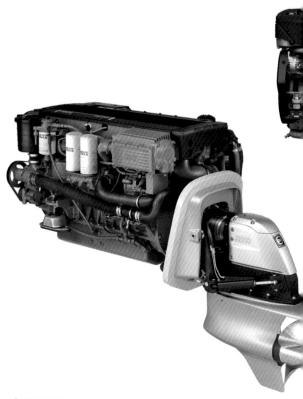

OUTDRIVE LEGS

Many manufacturers recommend the removal of the stern drive from the boat once a year to check engine/shaft alignment, and to grease the gimbal bearing and U-joints. This is a task for the marine engineer, who can perform pressure and vacuum tests on the unit to determine the condition of seals and gaskets well ahead of failure.

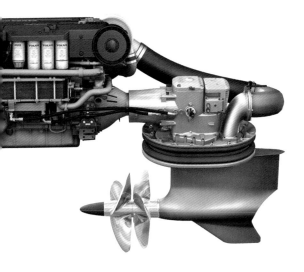

OUTDRIVE ANNUAL SERVICE

The oil should also be changed at the end of each season as part of an annual maintenance programme that should also include an inspection of the waterproofing bellows for cracks and puncture holes. The propeller should also be removed. The shaft can then be examined for any fishing line wrapped around the hub – the No 1 cause of seal failure. Grease the shaft to prevent corrosion before re-installing the propeller.

It is also a good idea to give the outdrive leg a pressure wash to clear weed and crustations at least once every six months, and check the state of the anode. If it has been badly affected by electrolysis, then replace the sacrificial plate.

Stern drives do not drain when raised, and should always be kept in the vertical, non-tilt position to prevent freezing when the boat is laid up ashore.

Re-installing an engine. It is imperative to line up the engine and shaft accurately. Add shims under the engine legs if necessary. Mis-alignment causes severe vibrations and can even lead to a bent prop shaft.

CONTROL SYSTEMS

Engine control systems, whether cable, electronic or hydraulic, all require some maintenance. If electronic, check for corrosion within the terminals, look for leaking seals in the hydraulic systems, and keep cables well greased.

- Cable systems that curve too tightly will be stiff to operate from the outset. Ensure that bends are never tighter than an 8-inch (20 cm) radius.
- Check for bent or corroded end rods, which will increase friction considerably.
- Check for damage to the outer cable. If water can get in, this will lead to corrosion. The only answer is to replace the cable.
- Check end fittings, particularly the split pins that secure the cables to the gearbox and fuel pump, and replace if worn or corroded.
- Check the clamping arrangement holding the outer cables in position. If these are loose, then this will lead to extra play in the system.

10 PROPELLERS

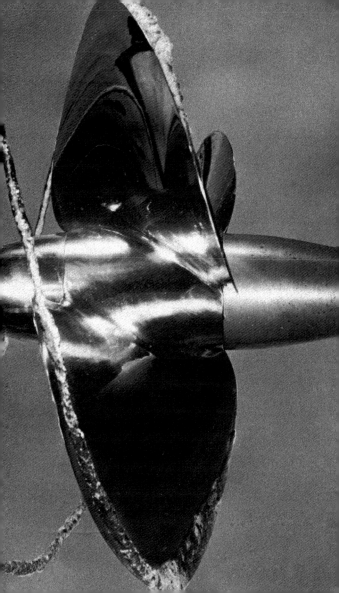

PROPELLERS

PARTS OF THE PROPELLER

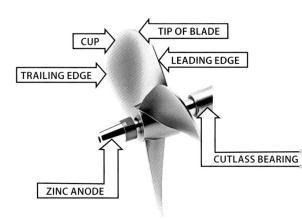

- CUP
- TIP OF BLADE
- LEADING EDGE
- TRAILING EDGE
- CUTLASS BEARING
- ZINC ANODE

CHOOSING THE RIGHT PROPELLER

The propeller needs to be matched to the engine and boat combination. If the engine is pushing a heavy displacement vessel it will require a shallow pitched prop to ensure that when under load, the engine can operate within its optimum rev range. If the engine is powering a fast planing hull, then it will require a coarser pitch so that the engine doesn't over-rev.

Pitch is the theoretical distance a propeller would move through the water if it was a solid. All props are far less efficient, even when new. There is the problem of cavitation, where pressure exerted on the water causes the oxygen to vaporise and leave a string of air bubbles trailing from the tip of the blades. The difference between the

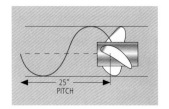

25"
PITCH

theoretical pitch and what happens in practice is called 'slip'. This can be as little as 10 per cent on a lightly loaded fast planing hull, and 50 per cent on a heavy displacement hull.

There are props that are designed specifically for work in weedy areas. The standard prop that comes with the engine will invariable be a general purpose aluminium one, but you can also purchase high performance props made of stainless steel and even plastic ones, which are the cheapest to replace.

The engine dealer should have access to a computer program to calculate the correct propeller for any drive/boat combination, or at least a comparison table listing engine size and boat type matched with the correct propeller size. This is stamped on the hub and is invariably annotated in inches. Thus 12 x 17 refers to a prop with a diameter of 12 inches and a pitch of 17 inches.

If all else fails, you can always experiment with various pitched propellers to find which one operates closest to the engine's optimum rev limit, as listed in the engine manual. The engine will require a tachograph, and the boat a speedometer, to provide an accurate guide against which to measure.

Start by making several test runs in calm water with the existing propeller to establish a benchmark, adjusting the engine trim to achieve the best speed.

If the RPM exceeds the manufacturer's recommended limit, then you require a prop with greater pitch. If the RPM is lower, then a prop with less pitch is required. As a guide, a 1-inch change of pitch will increase or decrease the engine's performance by 250 RPM.

The optimum is achieved when, under normal load, the engine reaches its maximum recommended rev limit, and the boat reaches its best speed.

11 MAINTENANCE AND WINTERISING

VOLVO
PENTA

Oljefilter • Ouufilter
Filtre à huile • Ölfilt

3581621

VOLVO

VOLVO
PENTA

COOLANT READY MIXED

Ready-mixed coolant
Kühlflüssigkeit - fertig zur Anwendung
Liquide de refroidissement dilué
Uso directo / Líquido refrigerante
Líquido refrigerante pronto all' uso
Fördygtandad kylarvätska
Koelvloeistof klaar voor gebruik
Ketervaeske
Käyttövalmis Jäähdytinneste
Kylarvätska
Líquido refrigerante e pronto
A usar
Αντιψυκτικό προς Χρήση

5L℮

1141674

MAINTENANCE AND WINTERISING

The largest task of the winterisation process is draining the raw water system and flushing it with antifreeze to protect the engine's cooling pipes during a freeze.

- Close the raw water seacock that supplies cooling water to the engine.
- Open the engine's water drains, the exhaust manifold and the turbochargers.
- Disconnect the raw water pump's outlet hose.
- Disconnect the discharge hose for cooling water where it connects to the exhaust manifold. Use a garden hose to run fresh water into the hoses to rinse deposits from the system.
- Reconnect the raw water pump's outlet hose. Use a funnel to pour a 50/50 mix of anti-corrosive antifreeze and fresh water into the cooling water discharge hose until the hose and engine block are full.
- Reconnect the cooling water discharge hose to the exhaust manifold and allow the antifreeze mixture to stay in the engine block for 10 minutes.
- Open the drain plugs for the raw water system and allow the engine block to drain.
- Lubricate the raw water seacock with white marine grease and leave closed.
- Change the engine oil, together with the oil and fuel filters.
- Replace the air filter element.
- Fill the boat's fuel tank to capacity and add a biocide additive to the fuel tank. Change the oil and replace the oil filter.
- Lubricate the throttle linkage fittings with a grease gun and heavy marine grease. Repack the stuffing box if necessary (page 92), and grease the stuffing box.
- If the boat is to be left afloat during the winter, tighten the bolts on the stuffing box until the normal dripping ceases. Tie a red tag to the propeller shaft and tag the throttles to remind you that the stuffing box needs adjustment before the boat is used.

Freezing conditions can cause a multitude of problems, even to boats that are well covered. When laying up in the Autumn, drain all water out of the engine and refill with anti-corrosive antifreeze.

12 UNDROWNING THE ENGINE

UNDROWNING THE ENGINE

Don't panic. This may not be as bad as it seems, but you must act quickly. The corrosion process will start the moment the engine is exposed to air, so unless a service engineer is able to start work immediately, it is best to leave the boat and engine submerged until you are prepared.

- ☐ Disconnect the battery as soon as possible and disable the ignition system.

- ☐ Once the boat has been recovered from the water, wash the engine down with fresh water.

- ☐ Remove the injectors and turn the flywheel by hand to pump out any water trapped within the valves and piston rings.

- ☐ Pour engine oil into the plug holes and continue to turn the flywheel to coat all moving parts and fill the cylinders.

- ☐ Spray the entire engine with WD40 or similar water displacing oil.

- ☐ This completes the emergency treatment. The remainder is best left to a service engineer who will have the specialist tools required to strip down the electrical system and replace the parts that cannot be salvaged. The starter motor and alternator, both expensive parts to replace, can be sent off to a specialist to rebuild.

- ☐ If the boat sank in fresh water, it may be possible to salvage the engine management box by drying it out, spraying with WD40 and re-drying before reassembling.

- ☐ The engine oil, together with that in the gearbox and any hydraulic oil, must be flushed out and replaced.

- ☐ Once the engine has been re-built, it is a good precaution to run it for half an hour, then replace the oil and filters to remove any remaining impurities.

INDEX

ACKNOWLEDGEMENTS

Grateful thanks go to the Adrian White MIIMS, Arun Yacht Club, International Institute of Marine Surveying, Monterey Boats, Motortech Marine Engineering, Vetus Marine and Volvo Penta for their advice and support pictures and information
Photography:
John Gott/PPL, Peter Bentley/PPL, Barry Pickthall/PPL
Illustrations: Kayleigh Reynolds/PPL